# Clever Charlie!

Written by Leonie Bennett
Illustrated by Julie Park

Rosie was having tea.
So were Mum and Dad and
Grandad and Charlie.

Charlie banged his spoon.
'Clever boy, Charlie!' said Dad.

Charlie blew a bubble.
'Clever boy, Charlie!' said Grandad.

'I can do that too,' said Rosie.
She blew a bubble.

'Stop that, Rosie!' said Mum.

Rosie wanted to watch television,
but Charlie was crying.
Mum couldn't stop him and
Dad couldn't stop him.

'I want to watch television,' shouted Rosie,
'but I can't because of Charlie!
Please make him go to sleep!'

Rosie turned the television off.
Charlie stopped crying.
But he didn't go to sleep.

He rolled over.
'Clever boy, Charlie!' said Grandad.

'I can do that too,' said Rosie.
She rolled over ...
and over ...
and over!

'Stop that, Rosie!' said Dad.

But Rosie couldn't stop!

Charlie started crying.
Mum shouted at Rosie,
and then Rosie started crying too.

Grandad took Charlie away, and
Mum and Dad sat down with Rosie.

Dad said, 'Charlie is still very little.
He can roll over, but he can't run.'

'He can't read,' said Mum.
'He can't play a game,' said Dad.

'Can we play a game now?' said Rosie.
So Mum, Dad and Rosie played a game.

Next day, Rosie was in the
garden with Charlie.
He put a leaf on his head.
'Clever boy, Charlie!' said Rosie.

Then Charlie put the leaf in his mouth.
'No, Charlie!' shouted Rosie.
She took the leaf away.

'Clever girl, Rosie!' said Mum.
'Clever girl, Rosie!' said Dad.

'Clever girl, Rosie!' said Grandad.
'You can run, you can read,
you can play a game ...
and you can look after Charlie!'